The Bronzes of Grand Junction

Other works by Richard Paul Haight

Tyranmatón
The Love Songs of a Lonely Man, selected poems

The Bronzes
of Grand Junction

National Library of Canada Cataloguing in Publication Data

Haight, Richard Paul
The bronzes of Grand Junction / Richard Paul Haight.
Play.
ISBN 1-55395-267-7
I. Title.
PS3608.A36B76 2003 812'.6 C2002-905186-X

TRAFFORD

This book was published *on-demand* in cooperation with Trafford Publishing.
On-demand publishing is a unique process and service of making a book available for retail sale to the public taking advantage of on-demand manufacturing and Internet marketing. **On-demand publishing** includes promotions, retail sales, manufacturing, order fulfilment, accounting and collecting royalties on behalf of the author.

Suite 6E, 2333 Government St., Victoria, B.C. V8T 4P4, CANADA
Phone 250-383-6864 Toll-free 1-888-232-4444 (Canada & US)
Fax 250-383-6804 E-mail sales@trafford.com
Web site www.trafford.com TRAFFORD PUBLISHING IS A DIVISION OF TRAFFORD HOLDINGS LTD.
Trafford Catalogue #02-0981 www.trafford.com/robots/02-0981.html

10 9 8 7 6 5 4 3 2

DEDICATION

To Korin

who by her sunny disposition and loyalty
has blessed my life more than any other,

and who, as a self-professed "theater junkie,"
will give this play, in her vivid imagination,
its most dazzling possible production, and that
is audience enough for me.

Contents

Characters

Narrator	A mature gentleman of about 58 years, give or take 7; an amateur local historian. He has a city "job" of looking after the bronzes.
Six females	of varying ages but mostly mature, each of whom plays (or reads) many roles.
Six males	of varying ages, each of whom plays (or reads) many roles.

At the director's discretion, other actors may be added to the cast, and some lines may be delivered electronically (e.g., the voices of 8 year olds).

The Bronzes (all realistic, life-size)

"The Woman With Shopping Bags," about 40, sits at one end of a bench. She is surrounded by several shopping bags, also bronzed. A trim, once-handsome woman; seems careworn and wears a dowdy dress and old-lady shoes.

"The Businessman," about 35, wears a suit and tie and snap-brim hat. Carries a briefcase, holds a cell phone to his ear, is in full stride

"The Pretty Girl," about 19; seems troubled, confused. Has paused to get her bearings. Wears s sleeveless blouse and short skirt revealing long, stalky legs.

"The Homeless Man," 40s or so; sits wearily on the edge of a mall fountain, holds a (bronzed) paper sack (could be booze) and is dressed according to the prevailing stereotype of a homeless man who could be a whipped puppy, a drunk, a romantic wanderer, a troubadour, or a serial killer.

"The Running Child," 10 or 12, with a mop of curly hair, wearing shorts, in full run – could be fleeing or running for the joy of it.

NOTE: Names assigned to characters are meant only to be suggestive. For example, TOWN CONSERVATIVE is probably rich, snappish, and mean, or, if a woman, rich, imperial, judgmental, and pink.

SETTING

Open-air downtown mall in Grand Junction, Colorado. In addition to the five bronzes, there are on stage a spindly tree and a large litter barrel.

NOTE: *The Bronzes of Grand* Junction is designed for full theatrical production with acting, sets, the whole deal.

Or for readers' theater production à la *Under Milkwood*.

Or for "pageant production," in which everyone in town takes a role or two – the mayor has a cameo as the village idiot, a local preacher plays himself.

THE BRONZES OF GRAND JUNCTION

SCENE 1. The City

NARRATOR enters with a large push-broom and a bronzed lunch bucket. He has a huge rag hanging from his back pocket. He is a mature gentleman of rumpled look and grumpy demeanor.

He moves about on stage as is appropriate and sometimes sits his weary, irritated soul down near the Woman With Shopping Bags or the Homeless Man.

He is also a man who savors each mouthful of words.

His other props may include a rolled-up newspaper, reading glasses to take off or put on for dramatic effect, a cane, and a pack of brochures, and a large push-broom.

He parks the broom and checks each Bronze, cleans something white and goopy off the shoulder of The Businessman, gives a perfunctory dusting here and there with the rag, then sits down next to the Homeless Man.

NARRATOR

(to Homeless man)

'Mornin', Onions.
Starry, starry night, eh?
Here comes rosy-fingered dawn
reaching across the Rockies -
gonna be hot as hell by noon.

(to audience as he puts his lunch bucket next to the Homeless Man's thigh and indicates the lunch bucket)

Had it bronzed - tourists think
it's part of the display and leave it alone,
my lunch - croquette of salmon

with tomato juice and scallion -
as recommended for "a creative and fun
surprise for your loved one"
by Bitty Schlegel in her cooking column.
(changes focus)
You know, in every town,
big or small,
short like Sante Fe, or tall
like Chicago,
sooner or later something will befall,
something comes sneaking around,
something off the wall,
like a bunch of corporate executives
running away with all you've saved,
or the ordinary Joe in your apartment complex
having unnatural sex
with boys he's killed and preserved,
or a checkout girl at the grocers
is crowned Miss Pork Producers.
Well, this is that something
here in Grand Junction . . .

CHAMBER OF COMMERCE SPOKESPERSON

Grand Junction is the kind of town
where an elderly amateur historian
can be hired to sweep the mall,
keep watch over the town bronze collection,
pass out brochures to tourists,
record local history -
more or less haphazardly -
and talk so much you want to slit your wrists.

A MALE FRIEND OF NARRATOR

Or be an illiterate old busybody
but have a weekly column same as Bitty . . .

NARRATOR

As you might have read last Sunday
in my *regular* column,
we've got a math teacher here in town
sleeps every night on the elaborate bed
of our most famous madam
from long ago, *whom* herself sleeps in a grand mausoleum
of pudgy angel and Greek-goddess décor
over in Denver.
There, her digs cast a haughty shadow over
the lesser mausoleums of the pillars
and pilasters of Denver society
of her day.

A MALE FRIEND OF THE NARRATOR

He calls that history!

NARRATOR

No, that's character study,
sorta reveals the tone of The Junction,
thumbing its nose
at the highfalutin.

A MALE FRIEND OF HIS

Yeah, agree. Screw pretension!

NARRATOR

(laughs)

Well, as I was saying,
this is the astonishment
that befell the Junction.
Here they are, our world-renowned,
gape-and-gosh-almighty famous,
strike-me-slackjaw, ain't it miraculous,
oh so mysterious
instant bronzes of Grand Junction,
living, breathing, homo sapiens one nanosecond,
bronze statues the next,
transformed, transfixed -
the irreverent say fried,
or zapped, or nuked -
the overeducated prefer "transmogrified" -
the reverent say transubstantiated -
right in front of seven eyewitnesses,
seven who saw it somewhat the same
except for a few minor discrepancies
of the kind you can expect from amateurs
startled silly by something bizarre
suddenly going blip ka-ching somewhere
in the peripherals of their very own eyes.

TOP COP

Seven solid citizens, if you ask me,
'til they went on TV.

NARRATOR

That's our Top Cop, who's nice enough

if you like thorny and gruff.
(to Homeless Man)
Big boon you are, Onions,
also a biggish civic mess,
what the old men on benches at the courthouse call
a royal carbuncle on the jackass.
Of course by now
the entire world knows
their real names and bios,
or could if they watched the news -
and who among you has not speculated,
why them? Why the Junction? -
as if there has to be a reason,
as if *we* don't *deserve* all this attention!

FIRST WITNESS

I've been hypnotized
and analyzed,
but I witnessed what I witnessed
and I'm tired of being harassed.
The God bunch
insists I heard lightning
and threw away my crutches.
The space-ship crowd just knows
I was taken aboard a saucer
by Munchkins
and injected with goofy juice
that made my gray matter
go Oz bodkins
and ooze out in little red shoes.

And the hoax conspirators
are sure I must have seen some guy
in a purple beret
peeing in the gutter
and expressing a lot of contempt
in French.

SECOND WITNESS

Should've followed my lead,
told it to a tabloid -
and you bet your best buttock I got paid!
Gonna move to Roswell
and set up in a double-wide
with my drive-tested new bride.
Laminate my tabloid spread
and hang it on the wall,
sell copies
and do-dads and trinkets
to turistas;
and you pay the entrance fee,
you get me -
a genuine eyewitness to history!

LOCAL METAPHYSICIAN

Hawking couldn't explain,
nor could've Einstein,
nor Saints Peter, Paul, and Augustine
combined.

NARRATOR

Let's see what mood our top cop is in

this morning:

TOP COP
If you believe the so-called eyewitnesses,
which I don't, we have here
a mass murder,
and this ain't no shrine,
it's a crime scene.

NARRATOR
Most visitors vote for divine origin,
magic and miracles being in the main
most conformable to the shape and dimension
of the TV brain -
I say in my usual unbiased tone.

LAWYER
The relatives of our bronzes
will be in court *again*
this morning -
three long years of litigation . . .

NARRATOR
trying to win
proper burial for,
or ownership of, their bestatued kin.

LAWYER
Just trying to prove that somehow, someone,
or some agency -

NARRATOR
with a lot of money -

LAWYER
owes them compensation
for the bronzing of their loved one.

NARRATOR
A man who claimed to be
the uncle of Mister Onions
was last seen
screaming on *The 5 O'clock News*,
"My nephew
wasn't no damn baby shoes!"
Meanwhile, the establishment lawyers
are genuflecting elaborately
before the altar
of Sorrow for the Bereaved Family
while stonewalling burial . . .

BUSINESSMAN
We must accommodate the thousands of tourists
who have a legitimate right . . .

NARRATOR
to form gawkers' blocks at sight
of bronzed Caucasians . . .

MALE VOICE
These are art treasures!

NARRATOR
Our local power brokers,
are nouveau connoisseurs
of art!
(indicates Pretty Girl)
Such as well-formed legs
and the realistic rendering of
(indicates Homeless Man)
"How Onions grovels and begs."

FEMALE SPOKESPERSON
Research shows that art
is an important factor in local community,
not to mention a benefit to the economy.

NARRATOR
So we are suddenly avid for
"cultural preservation."

WOMAN
Wish I could get a tan like that.

PROUD BOOSTER
Been two new brass-door hotels
drop in here
to house visitors to our preserved culture;
and a new La Quinta or Rodeway
pops up every second Tuesday,

NARRATOR

along with three more Taco Bells,
a retro hamburger joint with car hops,
and a couple dozen curio shops.

MALE VOICE

Some do-gooders tried to prevent
that Chapel of the Divine Bronzes
from going in
there on the corner.

NARRATOR

And surprise of surprises,
The Miracle-in-Bronze gift store
just this side of the chapel
is an enterprise
of the selfsame chapel people.

FEMALE

I hear
that reproductions of "The Pretty Girl"
are their best seller.

SECOND FEMALE

It took a lawsuit
by the mother
to keep them from calling it
"Original Sin" . . .

NARRATOR

Or "The Harlot of Grand Junction."

TOP COP

It's a security problem.
We get tourists with spendable income,
sure,
but also rowdy kids from everywhere,
you know, coming over from Eagle,
Minturn, Rifle,
coming here
wanting to paint the homeless guy's nose red,
or kidnap the Pretty Girl
and put her on a bed
in some tabernacle
over in Orem
to offend the Mormons.

NARRATOR

Top Cop is in frequent crisis
of professional restraint
versus personal moral impulses.

TOP COP

I can't tell you how often some smartass teenager
cops a feel of the Pretty Girl,
and I just go berserk in my mind,
wanting to put his butt in jail!

COMPASSIONATE WOMAN

Outrageous!
They deserve a decent burial!

FIRST MAN

This is their memorial!

SECOND MAN

It's historical!

COMPASSIONATE WOMAN

Give them a decent burial!

FIRST MAN

They're bronzes,
not humans!

WOMAN

(seriously)

Those are tans to die for.

ALL ACTORS

(loud unison)

Gro-o-o-a-n!

THIRD MAN

How long you want this to go on?
Even after three years, we still get overrun
by gobblers of the foreign tongue -
a German couple yesterday morning
and tour groups from France,
Israel, *and*
Japan
due in this weekend.

FOURTH MAN

You can't park downtown
for all the tour buses!

FIRST MAN

Don't complain.
Think how the profits for our downtown businesses
trickle down!

NARRATOR

(reads from brochure)

So why not plan a golfing vacation
in beautiful western Colorado,
and whatever you do,
be sure to visit the Miracle of Grand Junction -
our world-famous bronzes, waiting for you
amid the many shops and unique boutiques
of our beautiful, refurbished downtown.

SCENE 2. The Woman With Shopping Bags

A demonstration sign on A stick lies near the litter barrel. The NARRATOR picks it up.

NARRATOR

Nothing like a miracle
to stir up our local evangelicals.

The sign reads, "GOD NEVER CHANGES HIS MIND." The narrator puts the sign into the litter barrel and takes a seat near The Woman With Shopping Bags.

NARRATOR

So now The Junction is mecca
for the otherwise and occasional wise
come to gape and click and buy,
here to retail as personal insight
the daily TV soundbyte
or to decide with their very own biases
just exactly what these bronzes symbolize.

MALL STORE OWNER

They like our T-shirts
of the Pretty Girl,
but our best-seller
is the plastic dioramas,
either with flying saucers
or with angels . . .

NARRATOR

Take your pick,
a secular or sacred crèche.

TOURIST

(vehemently)

It's a sign from God.
The rapture is at hand.

TEENAGE BOY

(equally vehemently)

It's aliens done this!

NARRATOR

But hear our town liberal -
he's *occasionally* somewhat reasonable.

TOWN LIBERAL

Just as carrion hawks
hop gleefully from eyeball to eyeball
on the field of slaughter,
so fiends of righteousness
flock to feast on mystery
and fear.

NARRATOR

(overlapping)

Presumably the way thieves
flock to an unkocked door.

TOWN LIBERAL

Father Goetchal has brought The Truth to town.
In his brown robe
with its holy cowl
and white rope,
and his veins popping 'round his holy scowl -
he speaks with the moral authority
of confused sexuality
wrapped in well-tailored poverty.

FATHER GOETCHAL

Mock on! Mock on!
But The Woman With Shopping Bags
has the look of a sinner.

TOWN LIBERAL

The way Father Goetchal is adorned,
like a jockey,
with the racing silks of a martyr.

FATHER GOETCHAL

The way she so saplessly sags
toward the shopping bags
in an agony of guilty knowledge
is surely the body language
of a lost soul.
Could it be that this sorrowing woman
has committed the greatest sin
and had an abortion?

TOWN LIBERAL

Ah, never pass up an opportunity
to turn bronze into ecclesiastical gold.

FATHER GOETCHAL

Surely all can see,
hers is the posture of one
who knows she will be burning
eternally,
absent confession, absolution,
and the grace of the Almighty.

TOWN LIBERAL

The man adores statues of The Virgin Mary
and the cries of women in labor:
the sweat of women in the kitchen,
and the black shawls of women on their knees . . .

NARRATOR

(overlapping)

Whoa!

TOWN LIBERAL

(overlapping)

They're all so unclean and uppity -
women!

NARRATOR

(overlapping)

Let's have a return to civility!

TOWN LIBERAL

(overlapping)

Women! The cause of all evil,
and not nearly as pretty as altar boys!

NARRATOR

Hey! Gentlemen!!

FATHER GOETCHAL

So you see - this atheist is pleased
to play the devil!
Pride, or disease, has caused
his denial of The Truth
and his loyalty to evil,
but I forgive him,
as we must forgive every lost soul.

NARRATOR

And there you have our best,
and far and away our brightest,
at their testiest . . .
I'm glad I'm perfect.

COUNTRY BOY

Hey y'all - Psalm one oh four?
Thou sendest forth
thy spirit,
and they are created;
thou takest away their breath,
they die;
let the wicked be consumed

out of the earth.

CYNIC

Yeah, first God gives you breath,
then a glimpse of liberty,
then at some moment of whimsy,
answers your prayers with death.

TOURIST

Maybe being bronzed in midair
and condemned to this downtown mall
forevermore
is the real hell -

NARRATOR

I collect these homilies,
the daily commentaries
of visitors to our mall:
give us this day
our daily dosage of the conventional
original.

ART HISTORIAN

Well, in all history
this is our first experience of human beings
become instant statuary.
What are the appropriate feelings -
appreciate their aesthetics
or empathize with their humanity?

YOUNG WOMAN WITH CLIPBOARD

Hi. We're giving you folks a chance to vote
for whichever bronze is your favorite -
would you care to participate?

NARRATOR

I'm surprised by how many teenagers
get up close and start yelling -
'You in there?
If you can hear me,
move your eyes! Or
give us the finger!'

TEACHER

I had my students write a report.
Becky Bemis wrote,

BECKY BEMIS

(about 8 years old)

I saw some sad people crying,
but some of us kids was laughing
and wishing the bronzes
was frogs or airplanes
for kids to climb on.

TEACHER

And I was touched by what
little Passionflower Jones wrote:

PASSIONFLOWER JONES

(also about 8)

They were in the sun and hot,
like a car when the bank is a hundred eight,
and the poor statues
was like babies left in a car
with the windows up
and they can't move or cry anymore,
and their mommy is going to jail forever.

NARRATOR

Ah, have you met our local
minority scholar,
Abraham Falling Blue Feather?
After a long ritual meander
and waving of smoking sage, Blue feather
had *his* version of a conventional
original.

ABRAHAM FALLING BLUE FEATHER

This woman symbolizes
the materialism of her culture,
that brutalizes
and terrorizes
and empties her,
body and soul, into shopping bags.
Advertising on TV,
like Father Goetchal's religion
of original sin . . .

NARRATOR

A gratuitous slam, Feather!

Let's have some damned civility here!

FALLING BLUE FEATHER

Yes, of course, you people can instruct *me*
in civility!
This woman has been told incessantly
that she can only be
crazysickdumbbadstupid`n'inappropriate -
Oh cruel white-man fate!
She is searching in a Target sack
of heartless plastic
for the answer
to her every prayer,
but she can search in those wishbags forever
and not find the answer
even to wrinkles or vaginal dryness,
let alone flat affect or unhappiness
or *anything* serious.

NARRATOR

Feather is reportedly
an Oto
and is accordingly
discounted hereabouts
for being from a tribe
known for its sexuality,
this despite his BYU Ph.D.
in history
and his extensive training in psychodrama,
where he learned to say
"crazysickdumbbadstupid'n'inappropriate."

You want to try it?

ALL ACTORS IN UNISON

Crazysickdumbbadstupid'n'inappropriate!

VISITOR

I was reading the Gideon in the motel last night,
about graven images and all,
and don't bow down to no idol,
so even if God done this, it ain't right
the way some do
to go on their knees to pray
to this poor bronze lady . . .

WOMAN

I am this woman!
I praise God and care for my husband,
and teach my children right and wrong.
Everyone I know believes in God
and tries to live according
to the Good Book.
We are so belittled these days,
as if prayer is foolish
and loving Jesus
is so . . .
I don't know . . . !
It just breaks my heart
when nonbelievers
quote scripture
to mock scripture.

Do the cynics know
how decency and lovingkindness
can at least wait at the door
outside the devil's palace hall,
where blood runs down the marble wall
and Salome dances
to confuse the senses
and please the beast in man -
do they? Does anyone?

ALL ACTORS

Crazysickdumbbadstupid'n'inappropriate!

VOICE OF DOOM

In the beginning, God created heaven and earth.
The secret, bloody loins of woman
could not give birth
to so glorious
a universe.
Only the pure, reasonable, articulate mind of man
could accomplish so momentous
a task

WIFE

Well, it looks to me like she's just tired
from being all day on the go.

HER HUSBAND

Must be a virgo,
gotta go someplace
but can't find her damn keys.

WIFE

Reminds us how hard it is to be
a homemaker
and please some man and get so busy
it's news to you he's found
a homewrecker
who's a lot more fun.

HUSBAND

Reminds me how women these days
think shopping grows on trees.

FLORA

I knew her some. We lived on the same floor . . .

NARRATOR

That's Flora.

JANICE

I rented her and Flora rooms.
Nice, clean rooms,
furnished . . . I run a quiet place.

NARRATOR

And that's Janice.
They say around here that she could live
in a villa
on the French Riviera
but can't long enough remember
she's rich and doesn't belong here.

FLORA

Her name . . . *was* . . . Jean,
but she wanted me to call her Antoinette.
We were both Aquarian.

JANICE

You could tell she used to be
real pretty . . .

FLORA

Still was some days. She used to be
a dancer. A ballroom dancer.

JANICE

She always wanted us
to watch dancing competitions on TV
in my parlor,
have a party . . .
with Strawberry Kool Aid and Cheetos . . .

FLORA

She gave lessons until a couple of years ago . . .

JANICE

She'd spend a *fortune* to go to Denver
and see some fox trotter.
(laughs)

FLORA

. . . cute little Mexican boys
and skinny Romanian girls

whose mothers saw promise
in them, you know, as future stars
on the dance floor.
But the little boys wouldn't practice . . .

JANICE
Kid's today - well, don't get me started!
Jean said one time she'd had
four proposals of marriage.

FLORA
Five. I thought she said . . .
five . . .

JANICE
Flora! I ain't deaf. I know what I heard!
(pause)
That's one of my old dresses she's wearing,
I recognize the collar -
and my shoes gone to runover.

FLORA
Makes her look old.
Bet she was pretending
she was playing an old lady role . . .

JANICE
She was doing some shopping for me -
I gave her the money . . .

FLORA

She was taking singing lessons
at her age - vocal lessons.
Loved show tunes,
knew all the words . . .
lyrics,' she called them.

JANICE

(sings)

'I'm gonna wash that man
right out of my hair . . .'
She loved that one . . .

FLORA

(sings)

'I feel pretty . . .'

JANICE

(sings)

'Oh so pretty . . .'

FLORA

Yeah, and she sang with show biz flourishes,
puttin' on airs.
She always volunteered to usher
at the Sunrise-Sunset theater.

JANICE

Always smiling. Laughed a lot,
a real nice, genuine laugh.
So cheerful all the time

you had to wonder,
What's *wrong* with her?

FLORA
I think she had been, you know, intimate,
with men . . .
but she always had some illness going,
like saying to a man her kidney was aching . . .

JANICE
always advertising her physical ailments,
the way people smile
when they pass gas.

FLORA
Janice!

JANICE
Well . . .

FLORA
I think she may be the only one
didn't know her life was gone,
. . . passed her by . . . done.

JANICE
But people just keep going.
They rent rooms -
in Grand Junction . . .
I guess hope is more important than anything,

keeps you going for no reason . . .

FLORA

(sings)

"You've got to have heart . . .'

(pause)

I guess I have to accept

I'm one -

renting a room . . .

in Grand Junction.

SCENE 3. The Businessman

NARRATOR
Excellent workmanship, said José Villa,
the artist who made a bronze John Lennon
sitting on a bench
in a park in Havana . . .

JOSÉ VILLA
(slight Spanish accent)
. . . the Cubans are very honored
to have my John Lennon in their park.
They take photos of their children
sitting with John.
Pretty señoritas cuddle in his arms.
But your bronzes fill me with alarm.
Unless the artist comes forward,
people will believe it's an act of God.

NARRATOR
Our visitors have a genius
for analysis.

FRENCH VISITOR
(French accent)
These poor people. This tawdry culture.
To be rich makes Americans poor.

CHAMBER OF COMMERCE SPOKESPERSON
The French cannot swallow

that the quality of our local chardonnay
has superior flavor and bouquet
compared with their senile variety.

NARRATOR

Don't miss this -
ingenious!

FRENCH VISITOR

This society demonstrates the country-club model
of social organization.
If you can afford the membership fee,
and have no liability
of personal history,
or of skin color,
you may join and enjoy
all the privileges organized for you . . .

FRENCH FRIEND OF FRENCH VISITOR

But of course, "of your own free will,"
you will choose to adore
playing golf -
would you deny yourself
a benefit you have paid so dearly to acquire?

FRENCH VISITOR

And how you savor your country-club lunches,
so reminiscent of school cafeteria food,
but with garnishes . . .

FRENCH FRIEND OF FRENCH VISITOR

Crudités
on Wednesdays . . .

FRENCH VISITOR

And all around you -
nature converted to golf courses
and farmland converted to parking spaces,
a playground where members contend valiantly
with sand traps and out-of-bounds
and other discourtesies of artificial reality . . .

TOWN CONSERVATIVE

Don't know how we'd get by
without analysis from visiting foreigners
with envy in their eyes
and venom in their words.

TOWN LIBERAL

We do pretty well assuming,
as most folks around here do,
that common sense is superior
to wisdom
and the common man is better
than anyone.

FRENCH VISITOR

But do you not see -
your theocracy
and autocracy

conspire to convert democracy
to plutocracy.

TOWN LIBERAL

God is of the monarchic party.
Never did submit the Ten Commandments
for debate and amendment.

NARRATOR

Thataway! Let's *mix* religion and politics
and have another conceptual brawl
here on the mall!

ALL ACTORS

Crazysickdumbbadstupid'n'inappropriate!

TOWN LIBERAL

Janice no doubt votes straight autocratic
but thinks an autocrat
is a drive-through laundry.
Our Pastor Gooding and his Presbyterian congregation
may vote a straight theocratic ticket,
but, father forgive them, they know not
what they do.

"CONSTABLE" JEFFERSON

I never seen "theocracy" doing a drug deal.
You ever seen "plutocracy"
run a red light and kill
a cub scout den?

NARRATOR

That's our constable, Tom Jefferson -
the licensed voyeur of The Junction.

"CONSTABLE" JEFFERSON

The other day me and my partner
get called to a domestic disturbance.
We see all the front windows
are smashed and a plaid drape
is hanging out. The husband
is on the sofa watching wrestling on TV
with his baby on his lap
and his hand gashed and bloody,
as if that's the normal way
a man gets back in
if his wife locks him out
for having a few beers.

FEMALE COP, JEFFERSON'S PARTNER

His wife is crying and wants us
to make him stop drinking.
I see in the kitchen that its a mess,
so much truck you can't get in,
garbage, trash, dirty dishes . . .
gnats flying around, roaches;
so I have to tell the lady
either get it cleaned up
or lose her baby.
I'm like her mom
telling her to clean up her damn room,

and now she's got more to fear
from me and Jefferson
than from her scumbag husband

"CONSTABLE" JEFFERSON

That's what I call democracy.

FEMALE COP, JEFFERSON'S PARTNER

Every day
trying to enforce good sense and decency
among a citizenry
that's mostly barncats gone crazy.

"CONSTABLE" JEFFERSON

And my ass
if you think this don't include
the almighty middle class!

NARRATOR

As for The Businessman . . .

WOMAN

Prob'ly telling his wife on that cell phone
he'll have to be gone
an extra day . . .

TOWN LIBERAL

so he can screw
both wife and girltoy
simultaneously.

YOUNG WOMAN WITH CLIPBOARD

Hi. We're conducting research on social attitudes
and we'd like for you to answer five questions -
just five - only take a minute, OK?

VISITOR

OK, sure.

YOUNG WOMAN WITH CLIPBOARD

Thanks. The first question is,
which one of the bronzed persons
would you have been most likely
to share personal problems with?

NARRATOR

Our local progressive has issues
that The Businessman unleashes.

LOCAL PROGRESSIVE

(heavy sarcasm)

Making a beeline from the gun store
to the old gray Methodist church
that's soon going to become an art gallery -
you might say, running from psychosexual perversion
to psychosexual perversion . . .

NARRATOR

He objects to old Methodist hymns
with lines like, "Let me spend my life
in thy bleeding side-hole's cavity."

He explained this to me once,
but I'm too old for talk of sexuality.

LOCAL PROGRESSIVE

. . . NRA member, no doubt, a gun lover,
a gun addict, on his way
to fall on his knees and pray
for Constitutional literalism,
then home to caress his gun,
this neat man so betrayed
by the ignorance and bigotry
of the gun haters, so angry
that crime be gun-blamed:
Dear God in heaven,
dear Moses of laws and Abraham of obedience,
let there be justice
for Sacco Beretta and Vanzetti Kalashnikov;
and give us this day
our loaded assaults, our Magnums,
our snub noses,
our dum dums . . .

NARRATOR

You ought to hear him
when he's not feeling quite so benign.

GIRL

(referring to The Businessman)

He's really cute.
Nice, neat suit.

SECOND GIRL

If a man like that bacons me
I'll bagel him religiously -
(they giggle)

FIRST TOURIST

Neat and clean,
from the Latin *politus,*
"polished," "refined,"
like sugar and white bread.

SECOND TOURIST

Hey, man, that's his creativity
out by the highway,
the truck stop . . .

FIRST TOURIST

the silver-and-turquoise tourist trap?

SECOND TOURIST

The auto-body shop . . .

FIRST TOURIST

Krispy Kremes -
for the cops,
That motel - "Sweet Dreams"!

SECOND TOURIST

Hey, hey, it takes a businessman
of conscience and compassion

to provide low-cost lodging for Okies . . .

FIRST TOURIST

for whores -
with canker sores . . .

THIRD TOURIST

Seen one bronze on a mall,
seen 'em all.
Same for the Grand damn Canyon
and a Vegas phony Egyptian
from Jersey;
and roadside wooden teepees
full of ugly curiosities
like hula dancers with naked mammaries
saying Welcome to Kansas.

NARRATOR

So the tourists come and go,
speaking of aliens and sociopaths they know -
personally - and St. John's wort
and the high cost of travel comfort.

VISITING SEMINARIAN

We must meditate on the Businessman
if we are to understand
God's plan
for the life of man.

BLACKOUT: "God Bless America" plus The Businessman wrapped in the American flag.

TOWN PROGRESSIVE
I hold with Vico . . .

NARRATOR
That's Giambattista Vico . . .
never pass up a chance to say "Giambattista,"
or "persnicketiness" . . .

TOWN PROGRESSIVE
. . . human affairs are entirely human . . .
and God has nothing to do
with pimples
or dimples,
or DDT,
or amnesty,
or greening or bronzing a businessman!

NARRATOR
You through?

END BLACKOUT, return to scene as before,.

VISITING SEMINARIAN
The gospel is real and true
and says you're going to hell.

NARRATOR
Stop! You people!
You know better than to spoil dinner
or the Christmas season,

or a day on our mall,
with talk of politics and religion . . .

ALL ACTORS

Crazysickdumbbadstupid'n'inappropriate.

NARRATOR

Credit the bronzes of Grand Junction
with an increase in intracity irritation.

MAN

It's the tourists! You want their money,
you get their patronizing attitudes,
their bad manners,
their aggressive, competitive, hysterical determination
to get their money's worth!
and worse,
you get their plaid shorts
and pasty white knees
and sandals with black socks!

EX-WIFE OF BUSINESSMAN

We got divorced three years ago.

NARRATOR

I wish more people here in town
had heard his ex-wife talk about
our bronzed Businessman. She was one
who wouldn't go on TV.

EX-WIFE OF BUSINESSMAN

The best I can say about him is,
I still respect him. People ought to know
this trip of his
was to help me find a rest home
for my mom.
I know it's usually BS
that the divorce was all me,
but it was.
I can't stand to see
this man . . . the way he is.
He worked so hard!
But he was so sad.
That was painful to live with,
a man being a good man
but so driven,
so sad to be "average" -
average height, average mind,
Cs in school,
no way to be special.
No big ideas, Never a big deal.

NARRATOR

Was that it?

EX-WIFE OF BUSINESSMAN

No, not really.
He called himself "the Waterboy."
He was famous in college. He'd yell,
'Is the Waterboy going to score tonight?'

It was a big deal in the morning,
fraternity boys waiting,
then he'd throw up his arms and howl -
'sco-o-o-o-ore,'
and everyone would cheer.
After seven years
I lost it, about the two hundredth time
he crawled into bed
and said . . .
'Here comes the Waterboy
moving in for the score.'
Well, not now, nevermore.

NARRATOR

That's it?

WIFE OF THE BUSINESSMAN

No.
One day I was wandering in Rico,
in an aspen forest
on a bright, sunny day,
and I came upon an untended cemetery
in that untended town.
I found an ancient, broken headstone
wrapped in roots and thorns.
It read,
"This life had not been so hard to bear,
Sidney,
had you your thoughts learned to share."
(pause)
That was it.

SCENE 4. The Pretty Girl

NARRATOR

(seemingly wiping tears from the eyes of the Pretty Girl)

Men think she's possessed
about her effect on testosterone,

FEMINIST

but she's probably depressed
about a computer test
or obsessed
about urban sprawl,
or AIDS in Africa,
or the handwriting scrawled on the wall.

MAN

Then why doesn't she look
more librarianlike
and less slutlike?

THE PRETTY GIRL'S MOTHER

She was just a normal girl,
sorta average, got a lot of Cs in school,
I didn't know
she was home.
She usually called.
I thought she was still in Denver.
And really, it doesn't much look like her,
my daughter . . .

I don't know how you're all so sure . . .

WOMAN

That skirt, showing her legs like that!

BLACKOUT: Middle Eastern music, and The Pretty Girl suddenly reappears covered in black from head to toe - in the garb of a Muslim woman

READER OF RILKE

(making himself heard)

A righteous man barely gets his lust
locked up like a rifle in a gun chest
and down the street comes
fleshy tests -
naked bosoms
full of breasts.

END BLACKOUT: The Pretty Girl reappears as at first.

SECOND FEMINIST

She's a modern, liberated young woman,
unashamed of her sexuality,
the energy equivalent of any man.

MAN

Right, a prick tease.

INTELLECTUAL

Took us an entire century
to get over Puritanism

and another to get from Victorian prudishness
and fundamentalist terror of the flesh
to a genesis
of healthy sexualness -
so what if we've gone to extremes;
that's natural,
searching for boundaries . . .

MAN

Right, like the Romans -
read First Corinthians.

MAN

I put my faith in legislation
and the police.

SECOND MAN

Ever notice
how fanatics of free trade
and fanatics of free love
both passionately desire
that the other
be hog-tied
and crucified?

NARRATOR

The mother
wouldn't let them cut into
her bronzed daughter
to see if she, or it, is,

or was,
hollow.

PRETTY GIRL'S MOTHER

They think I don't hear
the things they say about my daughter.
I loved her. I always will.
That one about the drill,
and all the double meanings,
that's so cruel!
Why is everyone so cruel?

BLACKOUT: Wedding music and The Pretty Girl is suddenly a bride in white dress and bridal veil.

WELL-BRED VISITOR

Personally, I am not drawn
to pretty girls. I prefer crunchy women,
women who are subtly delectable,
like winey sauces and saucy wine.

HIS WOMAN COMPANION

Beware of the man who thinks of a lady
as cashews and broccoli wearing lingerie . . .

NARRATOR

or salmon croquettes . . .

END BLACKOUT, pretty girl reappears as before,

WELL-BRED VISITOR

I prefer the *jolie laide,*
a woman of unconventional attractions -
A moon-faced mountain climber
surprisingly lean and agile of body;
a hatchet-faced peasant girl of ferocious eye
who is a flamenco dancer;
a woman of insane hair and neurotic eye
who writes erotic poetry;
a freckle-faced, gap-toothed woman
who distributes food to refugees
and has unromantic,
but enthusiastic,
sexual intentions;

THE WOMAN COMPANION

Darling, your imagination has eloped
with your libido.

WELL-BRED VISITOR

(unable to stop)

A high-waisted, long-legged student
whose elegant companionship inspires
scholarly excellence; . . .

THE WOMAN COMPANION

Please. A one-eyed sophisticated pig
is as much a swine as any normal one-eyed pig.

WELL-BRED VISITOR

. . . a sculptress whose face is as *fatale*
or as madonna as she decides
you are worthy of seeing;
a zaftig entrepreneur
who becomes leaner and leaner
the closer to naked she becomes;
a woman of smooth, white, medieval body
and the spiritual intensity
of a temple prostitute. . . .

HIS WOMAN COMPANION

Thank you, darling. A woman is always flattered
to be well regarded
by a man with a rusty nose
and his loins in a truss.

JOLLY JOKESTER

You hear the one about the dyslexic frog
who prays
that a beautiful princess
will give him a kiss
and turn him into a handsome prince,
but so far his prayer has not been answered
by almighty dog?

YOUNG MAN

I'd've gallantly volunteered
to touch her
in all the places that give pleasure.

SECOND YOUNG MAN

She's asking for it, ain't she?

YOUNG MAN

It's a waste, bronzing a cute babe.
But I'd allow her bronze backside
to décor my bedroom.

WELL-BRED VISITOR

(to his woman companion)

I suppose these are the average,
boys who think of marriage
as entitlement to exclusive use
of some female's sexual assets.

HIS WOMAN COMPANION

I hear that the local habit,
when exclusivity is not granted,
is to shoot them.

THIRD YOUNG MAN

(dreamy)

One crisp autumn afternoon,
with a few white sails scudding upon
the blue surface
of the near universe
and with a playful breeze sweeping leaves
in crinkling waves and eddies upon the lawns,
I passed by a residential backyard
and saw a bewildered boy of about 3 or 4

sitting on a tricycle,
wearing a red and white cowboy outfit,
and watching his sister,
who was about 10,
running in circles around him
with her arms outspread;
and she was naked,
and so beautiful,
flying round and round,
so unselfconsciously naked and beautiful,
so free -
so unforgettable -
an image of everything joyous
and innocent . . .
a lifelong gift to my senses . . .

WOMAN

Pervert!

THIRD YOUNG MAN

That's my point.
I can never tell this story without
arousing suspicion about my character,
about my "prurience," my "secret desire."

FIRST YOUNG MAN

You're weird.

THIRD YOUNG MAN

Yes, yes I am weird - you know why?
Because I am no danger to any young girl,

or any other female,
naked or dressed.

SECOND YOUNG MAN

He's a wuss!

FIRST YOUNG MAN

So I suppose God bronzed this pretty girl
to keep her safe from guys like me,
the way magazines put naked girls
between the covers to keep them clean.

JADED MALE TOURIST

Hell, it only takes a few serial killers
and a sprinkling of rapists
to keep women in line.
It's what you call a cost-effective method
of repression.

WOMAN TOURIST

Yes, boys, we women keep our knees together
and lock the patio door;
but we go on living day to day -
in denial if need be -
but most of us defiantly
and bravely.

SECOND WOMAN TOURIST

If ever you looked at the Pretty Girl
with the eyes of a woman,

you'd understand:
a woman who desires to be desired
is like the revolutionary
who may win with bravery
but cannot govern even half wisely.

MAN

That's it! It's a weapons project
of the military,
Turn an entire evil army
into bronze statues.
Great for crowd control, too,
Get 'em all to stop moving
and making noise
and make 'em have to promise
no more damn protesting
or they'll all be melted down
for pennies
or little Statues of Liberty

SCENE 5. The Homeless Man

NARRATOR

It's man talk, you know, talking to this fella -
good mornin' Onions - familiarly,
kind of masking the way I really feel
about a man who's been through the mill.

MAN

I wonder where he'd been,
what he'd seen..

WOMAN

Wasn't from around here.
No telling what he was up to.

SECOND WOMAN

Just passin' through -

MAN

Kind of man, you know, been everywhere,
going nowhere.

TOURIST ONE

Just like any other visitor.

TOURIST TWO

Do they know what he had in that sack?

TOURIST ONE

What do you think, Glenfiddich
or Ripple? (laughs)

VISITING POLICEMAN

Maybe a Saturday night special.

TEENAGER

A blues harmonica?

REALIST

Probably a Dumpster lunch.

AMATEUR PSYCHOLOGIST

Was he going to turn his anger
in
or out?

OLD ROMANTIC

Could've tried to deal with his hunger
by coaxing a quarter
out of your pocket into his
with some poor-me harmonica blues,
(sings)
"I'm gonna lay my head
on a lonesome railroad line,
let the two-oh-nine,
pa-a-cify my mind."

CONSERVATIVE REALIST

Yeah, we call that free enterprise.

WORRY MONGER

Gonna stalk the pretty girl
and decide how she closes her eyes
for the last time?
Call that free enterprise?

SCHOLAR OF WILLIAM BLAKE

Perhaps he'd had punishment enough
to make him commit crimes!

LOCAL BUSINESSMAN

Regrettably,
homelessness and poverty
are the pesticide
and fungicide
necessary
for the healthy growth
of the economy.

MAN

(shouts)

Get a job!

FALLING BLUE FEATHER

Symbolizes the oppressed everywhere -
has fallen into the nightmare
of apathy, of hopelessness.
Like an overripe apple, fallen,
must rot

to be useful, to contribute
to the human compost heap.

POET

Is pulp of grape.
Is salinated soul,
deforested hope,
eroded imagination - body awaiting mudslide,
awaiting bloat in floodtide . . .

CYNIC

like ninety-nine percent of us . . .
one hundred percent of us . . .

CONSERVATIVE

Yeah, so, may you welcome his hairs
to your bathroom;
may he be a volunteer gray mouse
gnawing at your table;
may he be given dry socks and a cot
at the mission in your upstairs hallway;
may this refugee from the ethnic cleansing
in Utah
tent with his kind in your backyard;
may this illegal immigrant
from a poverty patch in La La Land
picket your patio
and stage a sit-in in your kitchen;
and curse your ignorance of the latest
in offensive music;
and improve your mind with paranoia;

and may your neighborhood
have its restraining order
against the exploited and oppressed
be compassionately enforced.

ASTONISHED LOCAL

You've rehearsed that!

CONSERVATIVE

I mean what I say,
rehearsed or not.

MAN

(shouts)

Get a job!

SECOND MAN

(shouts)

Get a job!

WOMAN

(shouts)

Bum! Get a job!

THIRD MAN

(shouts)

Get a job ya damn bum!

CONCERNED CITIZEN

He looks so beat.

Can you imagine having to keep walking all day
and nobody will talk to you,
and what will you eat?
Where will you sleep?

MAN

(shouts)

Get a job!

ANGERED CITIZEN

He's the same damn mystery
as the fat lady sobbing
all red-eyed and slobbery -
gets more disgust than sympathy.

(pause)

NARRATOR

A sociologist came by one day,
said he'd interviewed Onions -
at a mission in Denver . . .

SOCIOLOGIST

I was doing research for my dissertation,
studying transients and homeless men.
His real name, kind of unforgettable,
is . . . was, Eugene Tacoma O'Nion -
Irish. So all his life he was called Onions.
I asked him, born?

THE HOMELESS MAN, ONIONS

'Parently so.

SOCIOLOGIST
Had a chip on his shoulder,
I had to say, I mean, where?

THE HOMELESS MAN, ONIONS
Eugene.

SOCIOLOGIST
So I had to drag it out of him.
Oregon?

THE HOMELESS MAN, ONIONS
What the hell does it matter
if it's Oregon
or Paterson!

SOCIOLOGIST
It takes patience and courtesy.
Can you tell me about your family?

THE HOMELESS MAN, ONIONS
Yes.

SOCIOLOGIST
He probably thought that was funny.
I waited. He caved.

THE HOMELESS MAN, ONIONS
My mother spent most of the time
in a big field behind a Safeway.

(pause)
I suppose now you'll want to know why.
She was keepin' the field clean -
carryin' stiff yellow newspapers to the Dumpster -
and making friends with the rabbits.
(pause)
You like hearing about goofy habits?
(pause)
The other thing she liked to do
was get in fist fights with fat men.
She said a fat man
is a coward.
She had a cauliflower ear -
brushed her hair weird
to cover it over.

SOCIOLOGIST
What kind of work do you do . . .
did you do?

THE HOMELESS MAN, ONIONS
I got a sore mouth,
like a damn plow horse
with a bobwire bit between its teeth.
Part of a tooth,
back here, broke off.
There's a sharp point that's stabbing
my tongue.
It hurts to swallow, so I save up my spit
and don't have to swallow so often.
I'm learning to move my tongue

a different way so it don't get scratched
when I move the spit down my throat.
(pause)
You know you've got no manners?

SOCIOLOGIST
What do you mean? Explain me
to myself.

THE HOMELESS MAN, ONIONS
I'm educating you about being homeless
and you're restless,
waiting to ask me another damn question
off your friggin' list.
And I'm lower than mole pizzle
but you want me to *give* you something,
and you ain't gonna give me diddle!

SOCIOLOGIST
What is it you expect?

THE HOMELESS MAN, ONIONS
(increasing in anger and intensity)
You know what else? You'll think
I'm an uncooperative S.O.B.,
even though I just told you
this ain't me,
same way my corpse ain't gonna be me;
but just now, today,
during this one week,

my tongue is aggravating me out of my mind,
and therefore it's beyond me to be polite
to an idiot!

SCENE 6. The Running Child

NARRATOR

Girl or boy? That was the question
from the first.
And how old? Ten? Thirteen?

FEMALE TOURIST

Such beautiful curly hair,
blond and bouncy . . .

MALE TOURIST

though bronze and stiff,
as if
hair-sprayed.

NARRATOR

And somehow everyone seems sure
his or her shorts
are, or were, cockwattle red.

THOUGHTFUL TOURIST

Directionless, some say, a mad dash
from nowhere
to nowhere, chased by fear,
or chasing joy?
Expressing the freedom and play
of the unrestrained child,

all spontaneity,
running wild,
unthinking, unaware of street danger,
a stranger
to a world called reality.

NARRATOR

You tourists ought to know,
the nurse is persona non grata
around here - death threats and shunning.
She's in hiding in North Carolina
or Ishpeming,
who knows!

LOCAL

Got ten thousand, some say,
but six figures is probably
the closer guesstimate.

ANOTHER LOCAL

So we've got a profiteering nurse,
got rich off being a tattle-tale
and revealing the content of medical files;
then came family denials,
local outrage,
a decent doc forced to fudge,
and a tabloid headline . . .

NARRATOR

(reading from newspaper)

"Running Child -

Female with Male Genitals."

TOWN LIBERAL

Perky, born-again newlywed Debbie T.
told her fourth grade class . . .

NARRATOR

Isn't it amazing the details we pick out
to offend us, the aspect of an event
that gets our goat.
So when the tabloid revelation came along,
some wanted to run the nurse out of town -
tarred and feathered;
some were in favor of boycotting any store
that sold the tabloid;
and our town liberal was hot to vilify
perky, born-again, newlywed Debbie T.

DEBBIE T.

I admit it. I said,
'Your classmate has been chosen
by God
for a miracle -
to prepare the world
for the Second Coming.'

TOWN LIBERAL

Ah Debbie, so pure of heart,
so gutter-spout Christian.

DEBBIE T.

I answered honestly.
'No,' I said, 'your poor little friend
will never see her mommy ever again.
She is happy with Jesus in heaven.'

NARRATOR

Debbie T.
was history by 3
for not waiting until staff briefing
on what to tell the children.

TOWN LIBERAL

Never fear, her martyr's complex
was fully operational:

DEBBIE T.

I was only telling the truth, that's all.

TOWN LIBERAL

Her faith will keep her perky.
Her Truth will keep her simple.

NARRATOR

The children were seriously traumatized.

MRS. CORTEZ

(Spanish accent)

My son, German Cortez, a classmate, wrote down,
in his first spiral bound,
what was happening at school

and on the cartoons;
and every Sunday,
faithfully,
he read it to his bronzed friend until
(sigh)
I had to send him to Brownsville
to live with his uncle.

MRS. TEMPLETON
My sweet boy, Kerry Templeton, ran circles
around his former classmate
and tossed her a ball
every Saturday until he became too tall
for kids' games and heard a rumor
he couldn't handle . . .
none of us could handle.

NARRATOR
No one wanted to know.

LOCAL MORALIST
No one should know!

WOMAN
But the children found out.

NARRATOR
A classy debate going on here:
Religion says
there is some knowledge

we should never know;
Art says no,
there is no knowledge that,
for our own good, we ought
be kept ignorant of.

COLLEGE PROFESSOR
A national poll revealed
that ninety-one percent of Americans
had never heard of such a thing,
and eighty-nine percent said
it never happens.

ANTHROPOLOGIST AT THE LOCAL COLLEGE
I organized a conference here at the college,
where a Venezuelan colleague . . .

NARRATOR
From the perspective
of a local conservative: . . .

LOCAL CONSERVATIVE
. . . this "colleague,"
a stocky little man with scars zigzag
on his cheeks and a twig
in his nose,
a man with a geology degree from Sul Ross,
he reported, regarding genitalia,
that in his native tribe in Venezuela
the Running Child would be considered
a perfected human

and would be cherished and honored
and helped to be happier than anyone.

STUDENT

All you've got to do is consult
an encyclopedia: In Republican Rome,
it was considered an evil omen,
subject at birth
to ritual drowning.

FATHER GOETCHAL

I admit that as a priest and a man
I am deeply troubled,
but God's will be done -
and infanticide is even more unthinkable
than abortion, and equally as abominable
as homosexuality, and another reason
Rome fell, and when will we learn?
When will we ever learn!

LOCAL PRESBYTERIAN

Pastor Gooding can explain how God
has never, ever, been careless or deviant,
or been anything but compassionate and good.

LOCAL LIBERAL

So our scholars seek the truth
and our spiritual wisemen know it,
and I am horrified by how stupid,
and self-righteous

and mean-spirited
and vicious it is,
to claim The Truth for yourself
and go lovingly into the world
to bring all peoples to their knees.
When will we ever learn, indeed!

NARRATOR

The children also heard about
the conference, but
the anthropologist had tenure,
and it was his *job* to seek out truth.

ARTHUR

Well, he's either a happy little boy,
playing hooky
or a well-adjusted little girl,
running away from gym.

LOCAL PSYCHOLOGIST

When people are made uncomfortable
by overwhelming mystery
they often try to reduce the ineffable
to the crude,
or pervert the unfathomable
with the lewd.
I personally believe
that all mystery
will be made transparent for me
in heaven.

SECOND LOCAL PSYCHOLOGIST

In short, you sustain hope
with illusions and lies
and trusty old homilies.

ARTHUR

You hear me, Midge? I said,
He's either a happy little boy
playing hooky
or a well-adjusted little girl
running away from gym.

MIDGE

You're terrible, Arthur!
You're emotional bubble gum.
Where's the compassion?
Where's the negative capability?
Where's the love-their-prodigy-
as-thine-own?

ARTHUR

Life is cruel, Midge. Prejudice
is clean and unambiguous;
love is two-thirds
evanescence and loss.

MIDGE

You men are chickens cannibalizing your own
when they're wounded.

WOMAN WHO'S BEEN LISTENING

The more you men aspire to be
pure spirit,
the more bestial you become.

MIDGE

Pay attention Arthur -
she's right.

WOMAN WHO'S BEEN LISTENING

The more you men become defensive,
the more you attack
with metaphysical trashtalk,
and when that obviously doesn't work
you drown us in gore.

MIDGE

You hear, Arthur?

WOMAN WHO'S BEEN LISTENING

And ever and ever
it takes an odd child
or pretty girl
to let you know
your pants are around your anklebones;
but a businessman stands to make business
of your nightmare minds;
and though a homeless man with handscrawled sign
mocks your airy paradise,
do you ever learn?

ARTHUR

Don't worry, lady, there's always blood
and wedding gowns
to drag us down.

RITA

The child needs love, Fred.

FRED

The kid needs hormones
or surgery, Rita.

RITA

If he ain't in your image
he just ain't, right Fred?
You know the trouble
with Frankenstein, Fred?

FRED

Irrelevant, Rita!

RITA

He made a baby all by himself, Fred,
but he didn't get it right,
and it was not exactly
a compliment to his self-image,
so he didn't love it.
He tossed it out
along with his crackpot
Erlenmeyer flasks

and burned-out electrical doodads.
He abandoned his baby,
and when it turned into a monster,
it wasn't hugs, or math class,
or a cognitive therapist
that came to his mind
but murder.
And you guys think Frankenstein
will get it right
one of these days
and be able to go it alone
without your Rita or Eve or Mary.

FRED

You're a smartass bitch. Rita.

RITA

Am I off-base,
or wrong, Fred?

WOMAN WHO'S BEEN LISTENING

You got it right, Rita.

FRED

You got it comin' to you, Rita.

NARRATOR

When the family visited the running child
late one night
they broke open
in weeping and howling in pain,

and went on weeping when drenched by rain,
and sixty-seven percent of the town
finally broke down
and wept with them.
Twenty-four percent thought the weeping
inauthentic and inappropriate,
though the way they put it was,
"It was a bunch of crap."
And nine percent was busy betting on dogs
or, for all I know - gutting hogs.
At the press conference . . .

UNCLE OF THE RUNNING CHILD

I am the uncle of the, quote, Running Child.
The family has asked me to speak
on our behalf.
I should tell you that I am the editor
of a small-town daily newspaper,
so it is almost my profession,
as well as my personal preference,
to cherish freedom of expression
and freedom of the press.
Our family is frankly appalled
by what has happened to us
thanks to a greedy nurse
and an insensitive and brutish tabloid.
I believe it's true that children
can be cruel, and now we find
to our horror that this is a nation
of cruel children.

The correct term is *intersex*.
But you have taught my family
that it's an impossibility
for knowledge to overcome superstition.
Our family is somewhat grateful for those of you
who are silently understanding and compassionate -
and outraged and hurt
by those who have loudly mocked
and lewdly cheered
and shown yourselves to be
from the same family of imbeciles
who beat up homosexuals.
It is not the responsibility of our family
to educate you for common decency.
We have sadly been disabused of the notion
that this might be basically a nation
of good will and generosity.
We have discovered a land
of gawkers and ignoramuses
not even half a step advanced
beyond burning crosses and waxing windshields.
Though it goes against my nature,
no further communications,
no questions!

SCENE 7. The Citizen Investigators

NARRATOR

Oh how they investigate.
Oh how they write.
A professor of phenomenology:

PROFESSOR OF PHENOMENOLOGY

Of course I can elucidate
every aspect of this bronzing phenomenon,
but I will do so only in print
with copyright protection.

NARRATOR

Miss Mary Dona,
an astrologer from Sedona:

ASTROLOGER FROM SEDONA

I spent many weeks in the county clerk's files
checking birth and demographic data.

NARRATOR

No doubt looking for celestial houses,
and entrails in cusps,
and star-crossed coincidences.

ASTROLOGER FROM SEDONA

All things are written in the heavens;
these souls were ordained by celestial decree

to become bronzes.

NARRATOR
And here we have a practitioner
of violating confidences:

A WRITER OF INVESTIGATIVE GOSSIP
I hired seven private eyes,
and that let burst a cornucopia
of local legends, resentments, and lies,
like the rumor that the Pretty Girl
and the Businessman had spent the previous night
at The Sleeping Utes.

NARRATOR
And no amount of contrary evidence
or indisputable fact has put out that fire.
(pause)
And then there was the guy
who said he was an astrophysicist
but acted like a surveyor:
he measured every distance,
angle, direction, and hair
of what he called "the messengers."

LOCAL WOMAN
A psychic told me in confidence
that those "chosen ones"
with right foot forward
are truthspeakers,
and those with left foot forward

are liars.

NARRATOR
You can buy the colorful little booklets
off racks, arrayed alongside the postcards,
in all our local motels, drugstores,
and discount gift outlets.

A VISITOR
Do you think,
if you were going to bronze the living,
you'd select the victims
at random?

HIS FRIEND
Well, do *you* think,
if anyone were to create these bronzes
he'd choose the subjects
by chance?

TRUE BELIEVER
Never.
God has sent this miracle as a sign.
Our pastors and ministers will understand
and explain . . .

BYSTANDER
I'd've picked five soldiers,

SECOND BYSTANDER

five lottery winners,

THIRD BYSTANDER

five corporate CEOs,

FOURTH BYSTANDER

five bimbos.

VISITOR

It's some trick.
The magician kicked the bucket,
and no one will ever know
he did it, or how.

THIRD BYSTANDER

Wasn't no magician, an alchemist
trying for gold but got bronze instead.

VISITOR

Like at the Olympics!

THIRD BYSTANDER

(undeterred)

Now he's off somewhere cursing his luck,
trying to figure out how to talk us into
letting him have a patent
and make a killing on the market
making bronze of the homeless
and useless.

NARRATOR

One afternoon I saw a small man
with a large head
standing on the boulevard
to gain a peculiar perspective
until he was run ashore
by the Caddie
of a car dealer from Singapore.
He said
his name was Head.

HEAD

I have no answer, but I'm willing
to make something up
with the tantalizing ring
of plausibility.
Speaking Amerohistorically,
they represent, respectively,

(slowly and distinctly, with pauses. as if talking to idiots)

the commercialization of common decencies;
the genitalization of the body politic;
the marginalization of the callus-handed;
the subversion of the democratic
by the vertically minded;
and the commodification of necessities.

NARRATOR

I said I didn't see the fit.

HEAD

The *fit* is that,
sometimes, large words mean exactly *what*
they signify, and mean a lot.
Sometimes God and John Doe are wrong
and some seedy intellectual is right!

NARRATOR

An intellectual
from Chapel Hill:

AN INTELLECTUAL FROM CHAPEL HILL

If nothing else, your bronzed citizens
offer a rare chance to de-blur ourselves:
Look at us.
Take a good long gander. Is this
the end
that the vision designed
and design intended?

VOICE OF DOOM

The Founding Fathers exiled the king
to a space station in the sky
and gave him a permanent link
to his ministers and pulpiteers
so they can relay
his policy desires.

COLLEGE BOY

I learned in Human Geogaphy
that the nuclear family

is a recipe for dysfunctionality,
an aberration,
a tragedy for genuine community.

AN INTELLECTUAL FROM CHAPEL HILL
Approximately correct.
We are an atomized people,
assembling for bingo
or to go rafting on the Colorado.
We mistake temporary acquaintanceship
for friendship.
There is always someone behind us honking
whenever we're creeping along,
desperately trying
to spot the address
where we're late for a tryst.

SECOND INELLECTUAL FROM CHAPEL HILL
So what are you saying?

LOCAL CONSERVATIVE
He's saying that my neighbors
don't know it but they'll be happier
when they make my billiard room
a community center
with a sign-up sheet in my vestibule,
and when we all have a right to use
your snow thrower
before you do.

WOMAN TOURIST

Can you imagine trying to cook rice
and you're in a refugee camp,
and it's bitter cold,

SECOND WOMAN TOURIST

and freezing rain is battering down
on the plastic cover over your head;
there's mud smearing and clinging
to everything,
and your infant son is crying.

WOMAN TOURIST

Your husband is probably dead;
and you were raped by a soldier of a different faith,

SECOND WOMAN TOURIST

so you wish it was you who was dead.
Then your little daughter returns
and was too small and got pushed aside
where they were distributing food;
and your one bucket for collecting water
is stolen . . .

FIRST WOMAN TOURIST

A world of nightmare and lament . . .

SECOND WOMAN TOURSIT

bodies unburied, bodies piling up . . .

FIRST WOMAN TOURIST
a comfortless future.

MAN
So be glad it isn't you

TOWN LIBERAL
Yeah, lady, we can imagine,
the way teenage boys imagine war
and can't wait to go get an attitude adjustment
from a flamethrower.

AN INTELLECTUAL FROM CHAPEL HILL
The world that would be good for human beings
is nowhere in sight,
neither in the past of nostalgia
nor in the future of utopia,
and it's hard to accept that the world we've got
is only rarely,
and accidentally,
the world we want.

NARRATOR
Which is to say, I suppose,
that life on Earth is better suited
for dinosaurs,
since they lasted for 160 million years,
and some days it doesn't seem likely
we'll make it through this century.

BELIEVER

Praise Jesus! The rapture is nigh!

CURIOUS BYSTANDER

You praising the Jesus of unquestioning obedience
to a father figure,
or the Jesus of willing sacrifice of self
for others?

SCENE 8. Enter the Poets

NARRATOR

How the visitors do come and go,
speaking of nothing they know;
how the fiends of poetics,
the aesthetes and critics,
do mingle with the inarticulates
to engage in competitive aesthetics.
How joyful I am that I am perfect.

ART HISTORIAN

Just look at that pretty little tree.

WIFE OF ART HISTORIAN

How nicely it complements . . .

ART HISTORIAN

and *augments*!
this arrangement of bronze statuary.

WIFE OF ART HISTORIAN

But of course the tree
lacks just that irregularity,

ART HISTORIAN

that texture and *je ne sais quoi*
required of genuine beauty
and aesthetic complementarity.

FIRST POET

We have here
the farce of force,
military hardware
rumbling in columns of four
on parade
amid the bare-breasted dancers
of Carnaval.

CRITIC

A typical confusion -
mistaking the contents of mind
for what's right in front of your eyes.

SECOND POET

Sir, the clues
are too minimal
and way too banal,
and a limitation by the external
on the extrusions
of imagination . . .

BOYFRIEND OF CRITIC

You notice they're not granite or gold?
And they're new, not old.

CRITIC

So?

BOYFRIEND OF CRITIC

So, I don't know -

it might mean something,
don't you think?

CRITIC
No. I only consider what's relevant
to be what's relevant.

LADY WITH ROSARY
We pray for them every day
in my prayer group in Albany.

YOUNG MAN WITH DREADS
Mon, dey been brought to dis
by evil spirits -
tek more den prayer
bring dey back from de deads -
same, you know, for dem be slaves
and "coloreds."

SECOND POET
In the beginning was the bewilders
of may flowers and fondling fathers;
of pure tans and black hands;
of thievery by infection, colonel custard,
and the discouraging word.

THIRD POET
By which decipherment,
I suppose,
we has rounded into late-stage

self-reification,
of repetitive self-goofyfication,
with dervish cries of We're OK, We're OK,
yea yea yea . . .

FOURTH POET

self-inflicted embarrassment
by jingo-is-ment . . .

FIFTH POET

inseminating evangelization
and corporatification
of clonebreeding the meek and needy,
and papfeeding the weak and reedy
for reasons profitable and inhumanitarian.

FEMALE POET

the snootiness
of deludiness
of snoot lengthiness . . .

SECOND FEMALE POET

Never trust guys who verbal
the crude indelicate
and missionary the needy you
black and blue . . .

FEMALE POET

Oh yes, we're girls
talking like this.
We are the poets of no ess

and fresh tit for moldy tat.
And we don't trust
literal mindedness.

SECOND POET

(mocking)

But words cannot describe . . .

FIRST POET

You love truth? The truth is,
you don't *know* the words,
but they are out there.
Try harder!

THIRD FEMALE POET

The greatest evil
is The Truth
that must be obeyed by all.
The greatest sin is
vertical mindedness
that breeds righteousness.
The worst political failure
is insufficient paranoia.
And the greatest enemy -
the image in the mirror.

NARRATOR

See what I mean?

THIRD FEMALE POET

A poem should not mean,
but be.
Another brutal commandment.
But I struggle with passion
and intrusive opinion.

FEMALE POET

Imagine that you've been bronzed.
There is only fiction
in imagination.
No one returns to reveal that faith
is merely art
for pity's sake,
infrastructure for the sake
of the wake.

PHILOSOPHER

Do you ever feel a need, an impulse,
to make sense?

FEMALE POET

No. We've tried that. That's the way
of the monarch.
We are now forced to experiment
with the way of in-choate-ment.

THIRD FEMALE POET

Chaos has a more intriguing inner beauty
than monarchic reality.

SECOND FEMALE POET

And truth is as well-mannered as a cat fight
and as be-wildering as the psychology
of a rain forest,
as excessive as the energy
of the universe.

NARRATOR

And yet the friends of the deceased,
and some in the audience,
nod,
and some applaud,
without meaning to encourage
this verbage,
this rage
at the hands-off policy of God.

SCENE 9. The Philosophers Stumble On-stage

The Narrator picks up a demonstration placard on a stick. It reads: "DEAD FLIES AND FOLLY Eccles.10:1." He idly twirls it, taps the stick lightly on the stage, during . . .

NARRATOR

Even the visiting philosophers
provide an occasional conventional
original.

OLD MAN IN WHEELCHAIR

It is of grave importance
how these bronzes reflect
our collective intellect.

NARRATOR

I asked his name.
But no answer came
from the old man in the wheelchair,
only the rumble of phlegm.

OLD MAN IN WHEELCHAIR

(elaborate clearing of throat)

I see through,
not with,
my eyes, you know.

(clears his throat again)

I see through

the self-congratulatory anecdotes
beneath the umbrella of fireworks in July.

(clears more phlegm)

Thomas Jefferson speaks to me, you know.

NARRATOR

Really. Our constable?

OLD MAN IN WHEELCHAIR

(irritated beyond patience)

No, the Founding Fathers!
Put that down!

The Narrator obligingly puts the demonstration placard in the litter barrel.

OLD MAN IN WHEELCHAIR (continued)

Jefferson says that mobwits, to be truly free,
must cease papering over illiteracy
with diplomas from Virginia Tech and MIT.

NARRATOR

Does he? So he's your designated intellect
in the sky,
and you are his spokesman-elect
here below?

OLD MAN IN WHEELCHAIR

I see through the claims
that this is the age

of the lightning bolt. Oh no,
this is the age of poison praise
and the obscene bonus
for CEOs who require
considerable legislation
to help them behave better.

(more clearing of phlegm)

Behold the deep solitude of spirit
of these bronzes. Consider it done
that Grand Junction
will in time be desert without oasis.
But I see the survivors with open faces,
children of simplicity,
reverent, faithful,
and truthful.
By your unfortunate fall
will they become pious, full
of brotherly love,
giants of bountiful life.

NARRATOR

So you're a prophet, Sir?

OLD MAN IN WHEELCHAIR

I told you,
I see through,
not with,
these eyes. Vision sees
only the obvious.

YOUNG WOMAN WITH CLIPBOARD

Hi. I'm with the newspaper.
Today's Man on the Street question is,
Do you think any of the bronzes
ever went rafting?

NARRATOR

I tried to continue the conversation,
but Mister Wheelchair was distracted
by the Man-on-the-Street question,
and then, of a sudden,
my eyes were bewitched
by the intractable puzzle
of the wrapping on a tuna fish sandwich.

LOCAL INTELLECTUAL

If I may say so, some optimists pray
for disaster and misery
to clear the air
and make themselves feel right . . .
in the sense of correct.

NARRATOR

Ah, and here to further clear the air
is our local philosopher
of manual labor.

LOCAL LABOR LEADER

You might know
something like this would happen

in Grand Junction
with nowhere else to go.
But we've got
inarticulate mechanics here who can,
if they feel like it,
make a diesel bus cry uncle and women
who,
if they're in the mood,
can cry rock into biscuit.
But all this talk
is making them queasy and weak.

NARRATOR

A plumpish woman with brown bags
under her eyes
identified herself to me as among
the crones without an audience.
Yes, 'crones' -
her own self-identification

CRONE

(prone to fits of shouting)

You say,
the family of the Running child
visited in secret late at night,
and their tears
and howls of pain
won the sympathy of the town.
Why?
HAVE YOU PEOPLE ASKED YOURSELVES WHY?
Ah, the terrible secret.

Such a horrible fate
YOU WILL MAKE OF IT!
The issue is the structure of weeping.
The shame is in the observer.
By this arrangement of characters
here upon this dismal mall
we are told - IS IT NOT PLAIN? -
look! Look! Can't you see,
the child is HAPPIER
than the patriarchal heterosexual,
HEALTHIER than the postmenopausal
with her shopping bags, FREER
than the castrated wastrel.
And the child turns away, flees joyously,
has no ties to this bronze system,
IS NO PART OF ITS RIGIDITIES
AND TRAGIC ABSURDITIES! . . .
as yet refuses to be its victim.
The child is the potential Lady Liberté,
the child Lama,
who might set you free.
And have you listened to the cruelties
verbed upon the Pretty Girl,
how her own mother seeks to down her
to INVISIBILITY,
how everyone wants her
dressed and cooked and served
at the patriarchal cafeteria?
And there's the man, the focal point
of the heterosexual fable,

HERE WITH HIS FATHERLY GENITALIA
APPROPIEATELY BRONZED!
in rigor mortis, you might say . . ."

NARRATOR

And here my crone paused and lost momentum
and sputtered out like a lantern
going dry - such annoying futility,
trying to talk sense to such as me.
How wearying to cry
the same song from puberty
to senility!
(pause)
And then along came Sanity.

SANITY

You know what this is, these bronzes?
I can tell you -
corporate science. Drudges
in white lab coats, obeying their bosses:
'Formulate, for-mu-late
a tanning agent' -
one spray, psst,
instant color, you know what I'm saying?
Instant color!
That's what science does - screw up!
Overdo it, and what for?
Profit. Prof-it!

NARRATOR

What about curing cancer, voyaging

to the moon? Electric toothbrushes?

SANITY

Prof-it!
I tell you, if your witnesses had been sharper,
they would have seen the psst!
The psst of a scientific experiment.
And do you think a company scientist
is tempted to a public disclosure?
Not in his nature!
He's writing business proposals
and whoring to the Pentagon,
the C.I.A., whispering in the ear
of dusty warlords at the United Nations.
Got to find someplace where it's permissible
to harvest bronze from humans
treated with a tanning agent.
Psst!

NARRATOR

You think so?

SANITY.

"Think," sir, is the operative word.
If you people could think,
if you weren't so bereft,
if you weren't so blank-brained lacking
in paranoia,
occasionally you could figure out
just what is really going on.

And you think what happened to your bronzes
isn't coming over the horizon,
any day now, any moment,
to give *you* a psst?

SCENE 10. Guy Talk

NARRATOR

Some mornings our town psychiatrist stops by,
mostly to annoy me.

TOWN PSYCHIATRIST

Heard any good moral idiocy lately?

NARRATOR

Not a question I can answer yes or no, OK?

TOWN PSYCHIATRIST

Hey -
attractive women approaching from the East.

NARRATOR

So I see.

TOWN PSYCHIATRIST

Are you still using that cornball line,
"If I say you've got a beautiful body,
will you hold it against me"?

NARRATOR

There you go again with that yes-no trap.

TOWN PSYCHIATRIST

If I use that line,
it's therapeutically interesting;

if *you* use it,
it's disgusting.
(pause)
These women coming to visit your bronzes -
what would you guess, married?
live in upscale houses?
well-educated?

NARRATOR
I suppose.

TOWN PSYCHIATRIST
Clear skin, shiny eyes, permanent afterglow -
research says
they're in the high ninetieth percentile
for sexual achievement
and fulfillment.

NARRATOR
I'm going to ignore that!

TOWN PSYCHIATRIST
And one key criteria, according to the research,
is that they've all had at least five sexual partners.

NARRATOR
Doc!

TOWN PSYCHIATRIST
What, then, should I advise a society lady
weeping on my couch

for failure to attract her husband's touch?

NARRATOR

Talk to Pastor Gooding?

TOWN PSYCHIATRIST

Ah yes, pastoral marriage counseling.
Talk about moral idiocy -
our good Gooding
must preach an ancient patriarchal morality
to kids who will soon be in court
arguing over who gets to keep the pickup truck
and who has to take the baby.

NARRATOR

So that was the guy talk
I was trying *not* to think about
when our bronzes
entertained a visit
by the women from Cambridge.

Scene 11 The Women From Cambridge

FIRST WOMAN FROM CAMBRIDGE

If I had my way we'd be camping out
in pokies and dungeons
and collecting fractures
and honorable scars
and enduring teargas
and the truncheons
of cops on stallions.

THIRD WOMAN FROM CAMBRIDGE

(self irony)

Oh sure - what this country needs
is a lot of perimenopausal women
turning hot flashes
into political activism.

FIRST WOMAN FROM CAMBRIDGE

I was thinking tactically,
what it might take
to put a brake
on runaway testosterone "democracy"
and dog-eat-dog capitalism

SECOND WOMAN FROM CAMBRIDGE

(examining the bronzes and a brochure)

They're all so ordinary,
really,
I mean, they were.
I don't think I'd like to be

a statue, on display like some nudist,
and especially
spreadeagled in a glossy guidebook
as an obscenity
revered beyond believability.

FOURTH WOMAN FROM CAMBRIDGE
You wonder about those randy Cardinals
stoned in cathedrals
or bloodthirsty generals
on pedestals
in squares in Vienna
or Atlanta.

THIRD WOMAN FROM CAMBRIDGE
(gentle sarcasm)
Disgusting to think that one or two dozen
probably *deserve* our admiration

SECOND WOMAN FROM CAMBRIDGE
Well, don't most of us, when we die,
become knickknacks?

THIRD WOMAN FROM CAMBRIDGE
Sure. My Aunt Betsy
is dwindled to a small leather U of T longhorn
and a glass unicorn . . .
garage sales are funerals, really.

FOURTH WOMAN FROM CAMBRIDGE

Do you think death
is a punishment?

THIRD WOMAN FROM CAMBRIDGE

Of course it is.
You steal a single breath,
you go to the guillotine.
And if you're a world-class gossip
or bitch, you pass away and end up
at the mall
in a muddle
of credit cards and car keys,
your life for all time
orchestrated by Muzak.

FOURTH WOMAN FROM CAMBRIDGE

I keep thinking I'll do something sensational,
or at least a little bit meaningful,
later this afternoon, maybe next week,
sometime next fall . . .

THIRD WOMAN FROM CAMBRIDGE

Bangladeshis overswept by typhoons,
our supermarket produce section
out of strawberries, famine
in the Sudan,
crushed grandbabies and aunts
beneath the rubble in Turkmenistan . . .
and what matters most to me
is my niece's lesbian wedding.

SECOND WOMAN FROM CAMBRIDGE

I know. All I can think at this moment is,
the Pretty Girl at least
is not a bar girl in Bangkok,
or a seamstress in a sweat shop in New York,

THIRD WOMAN FROM CAMBRIDGE

or sure to become a spinster in County Cork.

FOURTH WOMAN FROM CAMBRIDGE

And I was never an Eritrean woman
too weak to shoo flies
from my starving baby's eyes . . .

FIRST WOMAN FROM CAMBRIDGE

And I never even once
voted for someone
who won!

THIRD WOMAN FROM CAMBRIDGE

My first instinct is to imagine
that the Homeless Man is probably not
a poet
or troubadour
singing truth with teargas on his breath,
piercing my heart with compassion . . .

FIRST WOMAN FROM CAMBRIDGE

or guilt.

FOURTH WOMAN FROM CAMBRIDGE

It's a shock every time I remember
I was trained to be a pretty girl.
I too had gorgeous legs,
before the wrimples and spider veins;
a little cotton
and I could live with my ballerina bosom -
. . . so much fate and circumstance
to live down . . .

THIRD WOMAN FROM CAMBRIDGE

I am so wasted by judgment.
So what if The Woman With Shopping Bags
had her hopes savaged by rape,
lost to indecision,
or was merely undone by a zit
on prom night -
there is no hierarchy of pain.

FOURTH WOMAN FROM CAMBRIDGE

Isn't your first instinct just some bias
or disgusting prejudice?
I have to treat my mind like a puppy -
a thousand times bark at it to *sit,*
to stop trying to hump my neighbor's knee.
I see a purple person and my first thought is ugh!
Then I have to double-clutch to get to OK, so?

THIRD WOMAN FROM CAMBRIDGE

And the Running Child -
cannot escape . . .

cannot escape our eyes, our words.
This angel child
was undeservedly exiled
to a great blue planet
that's heedlessly rolling eastward
horizon by horizon
until the orange star rises,
or one day does not,
rises above dolphins and anhingas
and beaches and elms;
blazes humidly in cornfields,
fires deserts into topaz,
inspires overachievement in hummingbirds -
. . . I-I forget what I was I going to say?

FIRST WOMAN FROM CAMBRIDGE

Sweetie, you've come unstuck from the everyday.
We love you anyway.

THIRD WOMAN FROM CAMBRIDGE

My mind is embarrassed by my unconscious.
I was going to say, Why wasn't the universe
kind to this child?

FOURTH WOMAN FROM CAMBRIDGE

Me, I'm so goal oriented,
sometimes I could pick up mercury
with tweezers. I understand this guy
with the cell phone attached to his temple.

SECOND WOMAN FROM CAMBRIDGE

We forgive you. Somebody has to confess
that the business of America is business.

THIRD WOMAN FROM CAMBRIDGE.

Sometimes I can see
the water of baptism
returning as the flood that drowns
dreams and aunties and whole towns,
yours, maybe mine
any day now.

SECOND WOMAN FROM CAMBRIDGE

This gentle summer breeze -
please,
don't let me say "rustling in the trees" -
may return to twist a village
to rubble and create
funerals and jobs, right?
And I think, Hm - how about that,
a baby's first word and a hurricane,
part of the same breath.

THIRD WOMAN FROM CAMBRIDGE

And the inexorable spin of this,
our bicycle in space,
makes us
upright even when we're upside down -
and we're so often upside down
when we're upright . . .

SECOND WOMAN FROM CAMBRIDGE

I'm right on the lip
of projecting my words
on these poor souls,
and I'd rather not . . .
can't help myself . . . I know, I know! -
false before next breath.

THIRD WOMAN FROM CAMBRIDGE

So many words
come into my mouth,
like worms,
to jerk me up to alien worlds,
visible only momentarily
and available only to awe and mystery
before I fall back to sleep
in my customary deep.

FOURTH WOMAN FROM CAMBRIDGE

You get an image like that in mind
what are you supposed to do,
have somebody rotate your tires,
or start the paella?

SECOND WOMAN FROM CAMBRIDGE

I forget - the way a faith healer
may forget that he's playing a role in a drama
and not exercising personal power.
And I rarely remember
that the sanitary glove

examining my soul
may feel like, but not be -
OK, I admit it - true love!

FIRST, THIRD, AND FOURTH WOMEN FROM CAMBRIDGE

Love!

FIRST WOMAN FROM CAMBRIDGE

This is a place of grief.
Every visitor must go home
and go on.

SECOND WOMAN FROM CAMBRIDGE

I feel gratitude.

FIRST WOMAN FROM CAMBRIDGE

What for, lady?

SECOND WOMAN FROM CAMBRIDGE

Not for anything!
The truth is, I sometimes just cry,
I guess for the same reason I breathe,
and right now
I'm breathing gratitude.

FIRST WOMAN FROM CAMBRIDGE

You mean now, not later, I know.
When Jeffrey was still alive,
I sometimes didn't desire his body
later,
didn't need his passion

soon -
wasn't in want of affection,
please -
because I was there,
free from when and somewhere.

FOURTH WOMAN FROM CAMBRIDGE

Well, some days I don't *desire*
a neat office,
I don't *need*
all my files in place,
I don't *want*
to see the top of my desk,
but I get to humming and just doing it,
and the whole time I'm all stretchy inside,
and it's like a blizzard outside
and all day Saturday in bed with Ted. . .

THIRD WOMAN FROM CAMBRIDGE

Mercy -
don't we just have one-track minds.

SECOND WOMAN FROM CAMBRIDGE

Well, suppose you're in paradise:
what would you miss the most?

FOURTH WOMAN FROM CAMBRIDGE

That's you. Maybe the homeless guy
would miss working on a pickup truck
and tossing crushed beer cans in the truckbed.

FIRST WOMAN FROM CAMBRIDGE

So you'd like to think that every human being,
no matter how wretched
or persecuted,
has interludes of dreamy bliss
or plain old happiness?

SECOND WOMAN FROM CAMBRIDGE

Yes.

FOURTH WOMAN FROM CAMBRIDGE

Obviously not true.

FIRST WOMAN FROM CAMBRIDGE

I'd hate to think any of us
has transcendent moments
because of the misery of others,
like missionaries,
or-or me, I guess,
every time I turn on the dishwasher.

THIRD WOMAN FROM CAMBRIDGE

The Eastern religions preach
tuning out the lifeless years
and making the most of the blissful moments.

SECOND WOMAN FROM CAMBRIDGE

Well, I'm sorry, but thank you . . .
thank you, thank you, thank you.
I love being with you guys,

hearing your voices,
seeing your eyes . . .

THIRD WOMAN FROM CAMBRIDGE

The way I felt about singing in the choir -
on tour,
singing *kyrie eleison*
to assembly-line workers at an automobile factory
in Nanterre,
knowing Paris was just outside the door.

FOURTH WOMAN FROM CAMBRIDGE

Me on the rowing team.
Just me and the river
and seven other sweaty babes
delirious with pain,
but I wouldn't say "unstuck" -
more like dead center in everywhere.

FIRST WOMAN FROM CAMBRIDGE

That
is all the tourism I can stand for one morning -
one more novelty,
another incomprehensible injustice,
all of us standing around,
numb and dumb,
gaping,
feeling useless . . .

NARRATOR

So, I suppose, they went off to lunch -
privileged and puzzled, you might say,
and me, to tell the truth,
thinking about their sex lives
and writing next week's column
in my mind - what am I going to write
about those women
and all these others,
these voters,
these wanderers
lost in life?

SCENE 12. The End Is Near

NARRATOR

Of late, no one has hung a crutch
on The Businessman
or a truss on the Pretty Girl.

TOWN PROGRESSIVE

Oh come again
all ye devotees
of novelties . . .
so we
can look you over
and relieve you
of a buck or two.

MAYOR

As your mayor
I must make known,
this era in Grand Junction
seems over.
The retro drive-in is going under,
and tourists are stopped in Denver.

FALLING BLUE FEATHER

We have heard the thunder
in the East and seen the tears
and candles on the mall.

NARRATOR
One of our Good 'Ol Boys observed:

GOOD OL' BOY
Usually takes a thump
upside the head with a wet raccoon
to get both eyes to singin'
near the same tune.

FATHER GOETCHAL
Now may we be one.
God in his wisdom
has clothed us in pain
and brought us to our knees.

TOWN LIBERAL
Now there's a thought
worthy of a twenty-one hosanna salute!

MAYOR
I don't want to get into that anymore.
I fear
our bronzes will wake up
in a jumbled roadside collection
of farm machinery or fishing figurines
somewhere in Missouri . . .

LAWYER
If you people hadn't been
so lacking in sophistication
and so full of blather,

so damn determined to drag your feet,
we could have had a real gold mine here
and a golden era for The Junction.

NARRATOR

Possibly so, but yes,
this is probably it for the Junction,
our fifteen minutes in the sun,
and all that will likely go on
for awhile more
is those rays of sunshine,
those rosy fingers of dawn
coming over the Rockies;
and each day we get another try
at being *human* beings -
you might say, a miraculous opportunity
to come alive.

END

ABOUT THE AUTHOR

Richard Paul Haight received a Ph.D. in English literature from The Ohio State University. He has taught at Southern Methodist University in Dallas and briefly part-time at the University of Colorado in Boulder. He was the humanities advisor to large-scale grant projects sponsored by The Dallas Theater Center and the National Farmers Union and was assistant director of The Colorado Humanities Program, a state=based re-granting agency of the National Endowment for the Humanities. Haight has published poetry, social commentary essays, and book and film reviews. At the time of publication he lives and writes in Denver.

www.ingramcontent.com/pod-product-compliance
Ingram Content Group UK Ltd.
Pitfield, Milton Keynes, MK11 3LW, UK
UKHW051130260726
13967UKWH00010B/2954